CELEBRATING THE FAMILY NAME OF FOX

Celebrating the Family Name of Fox

Walter the Educator

Silent King Books
a WhichHead Entertainment Imprint

Disclaimer

This book is a literary work; the story is not about specific persons, locations, situations, and/or circumstances unless mentioned in a historical context. Any resemblance to real persons, locations, situations, and/or circumstances is coincidental. This book is for entertainment and informational purposes only. The author and publisher offer this information without warranties expressed or implied. No matter the grounds, neither the author nor the publisher will be accountable for any losses, injuries, or other damages caused by the reader's use of this book. The use of this book acknowledges an understanding and acceptance of this disclaimer.

Celebrating the Family Name of Fox is a memory book that belongs to the Celebrating Family Name Book Series by Walter the Educator. Collect them all and more books at WaltertheEducator.com

USE THE EXTRA SPACE TO DOCUMENT YOUR FAMILY MEMORIES THROUGHOUT THE YEARS

FOX

Through woods where shadows softly lie,

Celebrating the Family Name of

Fox

And twilight kisses meet the sky,

The name of Fox, a whisper bold,

Is etched in legends, proud and old.

With steps as swift as morning's rise,

It dances through the centuries' sighs,

A flame that flickers, never dies,

The blood of Fox runs deep and wise.

Born of earth and stars above,

Bound by spirit, strength, and love,

A family woven, wild yet strong,

A heart that beats where tales belong.

From furthest glen to mountain high,

The Fox has learned to leap and fly.

Through winds that howl and storms that brew,

Its heart holds fast, forever true.

Celebrating the Family Name of

The hunters seek, but none can snare,

The cunning Fox with golden stare,

Its wisdom gleams, its laughter free,

A soul untamed by destiny.

The Fox knows paths where none have tread,

It thrives where others fear to tread.

With wit as sharp as moonlit blade,

In silent lands, its home is made.

But more than speed, or craft, or guile,

The Fox's spirit knows to smile

For family is its beating core,

A love that roots through every lore.

Through generations passed like trees,

The bond of Fox sways in the breeze.

A bond unbroken, unrestrained,

Through joy and grief, through loss and gain.

Not just the hunter, but the guide,

A guardian through the ebbing tide,

A name that whispers in the wind,

Celebrating the Family Name of

The Fox knows where the light begins.

With eyes that gleam beneath the moon,

Its soul hums out an ancient tune,

A melody of hope and might,

A call that echoes through the night.

ABOUT THE CREATOR

Walter the Educator is one of the pseudonyms for Walter Anderson. Formally educated in Chemistry, Business, and Education, he is an educator, an author, a diverse entrepreneur, and he is the son of a disabled war veteran. "Walter the Educator" shares his time between educating and creating. He holds interests and owns several creative projects that entertain, enlighten, enhance, and educate, hoping to inspire and motivate you. Follow, find new works, and stay up to date with Walter the Educator™

at WaltertheEducator.com

Milton Keynes UK
Ingram Content Group UK Ltd.
UKHW051141031124
450424UK00019B/1085

9 798330 497706